CLASS 43 LOCOMOTIVES

Andrew Cole

AMBERLEY

First published 2016

Amberley Publishing
The Hill, Stroud
Gloucestershire, GL5 4EP

www.amberley-books.com

Copyright © Andrew Cole, 2016

The right of Andrew Cole to be identified as
the Author of this work has been asserted in
accordance with the Copyrights, Designs and
Patents Act 1988.

ISBN 978 1 4456 5901 5 (print)
ISBN 978 1 4456 5902 2 (ebook)

British Library Cataloguing in Publication Data.
A catalogue record for this book is available from
the British Library.

Typesetting by Amberley Publishing.
Printed in the UK.

Introduction

The Class 43 locomotives are often known as the High Speed Train (HST) or InterCity 125, due to their maximum speed of 125 mph. 197 production locomotives were built by BREL at their Crewe Works facility from 1975 onwards, with the last one completed in 1982. They were classified as Class 253 or 254 units, and two power cars were used either end of a rake of MK3 carriages.

Built to a Bo-Bo wheel design, all were originally fitted with Paxman Valenta 12RP200L engines, which proved to be a hugely successful engine. All were originally delivered in blue livery, with yellow front ends. They were used on all regions within BR, and revolutionised high-speed travel in Great Britain.

In 1987, eight Class 43 locomotives were fitted with buffers and conventional draw gear for use as surrogate DVTs on the east coast when the Class 91 electric locomotives were introduced. They completed this task in 1991, and were put back into normal service, still retaining their buffers. Today, six of these locomotives are in use with Grand Central, while the remaining two were used by Network Rail on their New Measurement Train.

A re-engine programme was to be undertaken, with four being experimentally fitted with Mirrlees Blackstone MB190 engines – although these particular engines were never fitted to the class *en masse*. A small number of the class were fitted with Paxman 12VP185 engines, and today these locomotives form the East Midlands Trains fleet working out of London St Pancras. The remaining locomotives were fitted with MTU 16V4000 engines and all were renumbered, with '200' added to their original number series – except for the Great Western fleet, which retained their original numbers. The renumbered locomotives work for CrossCountry, Grand Central and Virgin Trains East Coast.

All 197 locomotives are still in use today, with three exceptions, which resulted from power cars being scrapped following high-profile accidents.

Ladbroke Grove, Ufton Nervet and the Southall accidents claimed power cars Nos 43011, 43019 and 43173, with all three being scrapped.

A replacement train has been announced for the Great Western and East Coast fleet, with Hitachi building their Super Express Trains, which will replace the Class 43s on the Great Western and East Coast route within a few years. As yet, there are no replacements on order for the remaining fleets.

A fleet of nineteen power cars was built for Australian operator CountryLink for long-distance trains in Australia from 1981 onwards by Comeng. All were originally fitted with the Paxman Valenta engines, but the Paxman VP185, as used in the East Midlands fleet, has replaced these. All are in use still today, but the operator is now known as NSW TrainLink.

I hope you enjoy looking through this collection of photographs, which charts the career of a remarkable locomotive class – one which continues to see mainline service today.

No. 41001, 6 August 2000

No. 41001 is seen on display at Old Oak Common open day, 2000. This was one of two prototype locomotives built at Crewe Works in 1972, and carries set number 252001. Both locos were taken into departmental stock when they had finished their testing: No. 41001 was preserved, whereas No. 41002 was scrapped. They were the forerunners to the Class 43 locomotives.

No. 43002, 18 September 1999

No. 43002 stands at Exeter St Davids with a Great Western working towards the southwest. This loco carries the name *Techniquest*, and has also carried the name *Top of the Pops*. It carries the first version of Great Western livery following privatisation.

No. 43004, 30 August 2001

No. 43004 is seen at Plymouth carrying the second version of First Great Western livery. It has just been uncoupled from a High Speed Train set, and was on its way to Laira for repairs. No. 43004 carries the name *Borough of Swindon*, but has also carried the name *Swan Hunter*.

No. 43005, 12 October 1998

No. 43005 is seen waiting to depart from Plymouth with a working towards London Paddington, and is carrying the first version of Great Western livery.

No. 43006, 23 March 1985

No. 43006 is seen at London Paddington in the original InterCity 125 blue-and-yellow livery. These trains have a power car at either end to eliminate the need for the engine to run round. No. 43006 has since been renumbered as 43206, following the fitting of an MTU power unit, and operates on the east coast.

No. 43011, 30 June 1999

No. 43011 is seen receiving attention at London Paddington, carrying the name *Reader 125*. It was withdrawn from service following the Ladbroke Grove accident in 1999, becoming one of only three Class 43 locomotives to be scrapped; this was completed in 2002.

No. 43013, 18 September 2012

No. 43013 is seen on the back of a Network Rail Measurement Train at Nuneaton. This power car is fitted with buffers and draw gear from when it was used as a surrogate DVT on the east coast, when the Class 91 locomotives were introduced. It carries Network Rail yellow livery.

No. 43013, 20 September 1996

No. 43013 is seen working through Kensington Olympia, carrying InterCity Swallow livery. It carries the name *Cross Country Voyager*, a name it only carried for just over two years. It later passed to Network Rail for use on Measurement Trains.

No. 43014, 18 September 2012

No. 43014 enters Nuneaton station with a Network Rail New Measurement Train. This had passed to Network Rail from Virgin Trains, and is fitted with buffers and draw gear. Other additions for its role with Network Rail include an extra headlight above the windscreen, and a box, just underneath the windscreen, containing a forward-facing video camera.

No. 43015, 11 April 1990

No. 43015 is seen departing Derby station, carrying InterCity swallow livery, with a working towards Birmingham New Street. Of note is the smashed windscreen; the train continued in this fashion.

No. 43016, 17 November 2008
No. 43016 is seen at Bristol Temple Meads, having arrived on the back of a working from London Paddington. This loco carries plain First Great Western blue livery and, by this time, had been fitted with a new MTU engine in place of its Paxman Valenta power unit.

No. 43017, 1 August 2002
No. 43017 is seen at Exeter St Davids, carrying First Great Western blue livery with white around the front. The white was later replaced with blue. This once carried the name *HTV West*.

No. 43018, 2 April 2009

No. 43018 is seen at Bristol Temple Meads carrying blue First Great Western livery. This livery was applied to the locomotives when they had received their MTU power units at Brush, Loughborough. This once carried the name *The Red Cross*.

No. 43019, 9 June 2000

No. 43019 sits at Plymouth station, having arrived from London Paddington carrying the second version of First Great Western livery with the gold band. This power car carries the name *Dinas Abertawe / City of Swansea*. This was another Class 43 to be withdrawn following collision damage; this time due to involvement in the Ufton Nervet accident. It was scrapped by Sims Metals, Beeston, in July 2005.

No. 43020, 12 March 2015

No. 43020 stands on the buffers at London Paddington carrying blue First Great Western livery. This loco carries the name *MTU Power, Passion, Partnership*, and has been plying the Great Western route for nearly forty years.

No. 43021, 8 June 1980

No. 43021 stands at Swindon station carrying the original InterCity 125 blue and yellow livery, complete with 253010 set number on the front. This had been in service for only four years.

No. 43022, 1 June 2000

No. 43022 stands at Exeter St Davids carrying First Great Western livery with the gold band.

No. 43023, 22 August 1987

No. 43023 is seen departing Reading station, carrying InterCity executive livery complete with set number 253011 on the front. The set numbers were only carried for a while before they were removed.

No. 43023, 20 August 1998

No. 43023 stands at Plymouth station having arrived from London Paddington. It carries the first version of Great Western livery. This once carried the name *County of Cornwall*.

No. 43024, 12 March 2015

No. 43024 arrives at London Paddington carrying blue First Great Western livery, and the name *Great Western Society 1961–2011 Didcot Railway Centre*.

No. 43025, 20 August 1998

No. 43025 is seen waiting to depart Plymouth station, carrying the first version of Great Western livery. The loco carries the name *Exeter*.

No. 43027, 3 September 2005

No. 43027 stands at Newton Abbott, carrying First Great Western blue livery with the big gold First logo. This carries the name *Glorious Devon*, a name it still has to this day.

No. 43028, 31 August 1999

No. 43028 is seen at Newport with a Great Western working towards Cardiff Central. It carries First Great Western livery with the gold band.

No. 43029, 31 August 2000

No. 43029 is seen at Exeter St Davids carrying unbranded InterCity swallow livery. This was one of the last to carry this livery, and it is seen coupled to a rake of Virgin Trains MK3 carriages. No. 43029 would move to First Great Western, and became the first power car to receive the First blue livery with the white front.

No. 43032, 3 August 2002

No. 43032 is seen at Paignton, carrying First Great Western blue livery with the white front. This power car carries the name *The Royal Regiment of Wales*.

No. 43033, 2 April 2009

No. 43033 arrives at Bristol Temple Meads with a terminating service from London Paddington. This carries plain First Great Western blue livery, and the name *Driver Brian Cooper 15th June 1947 – 5th October 1999*. Cooper was at the controls of No. 43011 when it was involved in the Ladbroke Grove accident, losing his life in the process.

No. 43034, 17 November 2008

No. 43034 is seen at Cardiff Central, carrying the blue First Great Western livery it received when it gained its MTU engine at Brush, Loughborough. It also carries the name *Travelwatch SouthWest*.

No. 43036, 10 August 1992

No. 43036 is seen on one of the centre roads at Plymouth before coupling to the rake of MK3 carriages to the right. This power-car change used to happen regularly at Plymouth, with defective power cars heading for nearby Laira depot.

No. 43038, 13 June 1990

No. 43038 is seen arriving at Leicester with a working from London St Pancras, carrying InterCity swallow livery. This power car was unique in having the full-yellow front end and white roof; although the power cars fitted with buffers had the full-yellow front, they had a yellow cab roof as well. No. 43038 has since been renumbered as 43238 following the fitting of an MTU engine.

No. 43039, 27 May 1987

No. 43039 is seen passing Saltley depot, Birmingham, carrying InterCity executive livery on the back of a rake of blue and grey MK3 carriages heading to the northeast. No. 43039 now carries the number 43239, having had an MTU engine fitted.

No. 43039, 23 August 2007

No. 43039 arrives at Doncaster carrying GNER blue livery, with a matching rake of Mk3 carriages. Of note is the advert on the side for discount online fares. This livery sat very nicely on the Class 43 power cars. No. 43039 now carries the number 43239, and still operates on the east coast.

No. 43040, 10 August 1990

No. 43040 is seen departing Leicester, carrying a fresh coat of InterCity swallow livery. It had been named *Granite City* just six weeks prior at Aberdeen.

No. 43042, 25 August 1988

No. 43042 is seen passing through Peterborough station on one of the through roads, carrying InterCity executive livery, and also carries its running number on the front.

No. 43043, 11 August 1997

No. 43043 is seen waiting to depart from London St Pancras, carrying newly applied Midland Mainline teal livery. This scene has since changed beyond all recognition, with the station now used for Eurostar departures to the continent. No. 43043 carries the name *Leicestershire County Cricket Club*.

No. 43045, 18 August 1984

No. 43045 is seen making a station call at Doncaster, carrying original InterCity 125 blue-and-yellow livery. It also carries the name *The Grammar School Doncaster AD1350.*

No. 43045, 31 December 2012

No. 43045 is seen at Derby station, carrying the current East Midlands Trains blue-and-white livery. The East Midlands fleet of Class 43 power cars were fitted with Paxman VP185 engines instead of the MTU power units that were fitted to most other power cars.

No. 43047, 12 May 2004

No. 43047 is seen passing behind Derby station, carrying Midland Mainline teal livery. The power car is attached to a rake of former Virgin Trains MK3 carriages, which had transferred to Midland Mainline. No. 43047 once carried the name *Rotherham Enterprise* when it was based on the east coast.

No. 43047, 29 January 2013

No. 43047 is seen arriving at Leicester, carrying East Midlands Trains livery with a working to London St Pancras. The Class 43 power cars helped eliminate Class 45s and Class 47s from the Midland Mainline route when they were introduced.

No. 43049, 11 August 1997

No. 43049 is seen departing London St Pancras carrying the name *Neville Hill*. Of note is the fact that the Mk3 carriages are still carrying InterCity livery.

No. 43049, 27 March 1998

No. 43049 is seen having arrived at London St Pancras, carrying Midland Mainline teal livery. This carries the name *Neville Hill*, and is seen complete with a 'not to be moved' board attached.

No. 43049, 31 December 2012

No. 43049 is seen at Derby carrying East Midlands Trains livery, complete with the name *Neville Hill*, which it has carried for over thirty years.

No. 43052, 29 January 2013

No. 43052 is seen carrying East Midlands Trains livery at Nottingham as it waits to depart for London St Pancras.

No. 43056, 21 June 1999

No. 43056 departs Derby with a Midland Mainline working to London St Pancras. No. 43056 carries Midland Mainline livery, and this colour scheme looked really good on the Class 43s.

No. 43058, 17 May 1997

No. 43058 departs London St Pancras carrying Midland Mainline teal livery, and also carries the name *Midland Pride*.

No. 43062, 2 May 2004
No. 43062 stands at Derby wearing Network Rail New Measurement Train yellow livery. This is one of three Class 43 locomotives that are used in this role, Nos 43013 and 43014 being the other two.

No. 43062, 22 April 2009
No. 43062 is seen passing Washwood Heath on Network Rail Measurement Train duties. The three Class 43s on these duties are a familiar sight across the network. The loco had been named *John Armitt* by this time.

No. 43064, 13 April 1985

No. 43064 is seen inside Derby Works while undergoing overhaul. This view shows how the front lifts up to allow the loco to be moved around. The loco carries InterCity executive livery and also the name *City of York*.

No. 43065, 1 March 1988

No. 43065 is seen passing Washwood Heath, being propelled back towards Saltley by No. 56071 following sideswipe damage. It would spend a few days on Saltley before going off for repair, and was later converted to a surrogate DVT for Class 91 workings.

No. 43065, 27 May 1998

No. 43065 stands at Warrington Bank Quay wearing InterCity swallow livery. This view shows the buffers fitted when it was on Class 91 workings on the east coast, before the Mk4 DVTs came on stream. It also carries the name *City of Edinburgh*.

No. 43066, 13 June 1998

No. 43066 *Nottingham Playhouse* is seen standing at Sheffield station, waiting to depart with a Midland Mainline working to London St Pancras.

No. 43067, 30 August 1996

No. 43067 is seen waiting to depart from Carlisle station to the south, while carrying InterCity swallow livery. This is another buffer-fitted example, of which six would find use with Grand Central, and the remaining two would pass to Network Rail.

No. 43067, 27 November 2008

No. 43067 arrives at London King's Cross wearing the original Grand Central black livery. This is before the loco was fitted with an MTU engine, as it still retains its original number; it became No. 43467 upon conversion.

No. 43068, 28 May 1998

No. 43068 is seen making a station call at Stafford while working for Virgin Trains CrossCountry. This power car was named *The Red Nose*, and also carries the XC logos on the side, which were removed shortly afterwards. This later passed to Grand Central.

No. 43069, 17 November 2008

No. 43069 is seen arriving at Cardiff Central, carrying First Great Western blue livery. This livery was applied when the loco received its MTU engine at Brush Loughborough.

No. 43070, 30 March 1997

No. 43070 is seen on the rear of a HST working at Thirsk, on the East Coast Main Line, while still carrying InterCity swallow livery. Today, Virgin Trains East Coast and CrossCountry Class 43s still work through Thirsk.

Nos 43071 and 43065, 9 May 2000

Nos 43071 and 43065 are seen coupled back to back at Plymouth, about to perform a power-car swap on a Virgin Trains CrossCountry working. This operation happened quite regularly at Plymouth, with defective power cars heading for nearby Laira depot.

Nos 43071 and 43029, 2 June 2000

Nos 43071 and 43029 are seen passing at Exeter St Davids. Despite privatisation having been running for four years, both still retain InterCity swallow livery.

No. 43071, 22 May 2008

No. 43071 is seen at Bristol Temple Meads having arrived on the back of a terminating service from London Paddington. It carries First Great Western blue livery, indicating that it had been fitted with an MTU power unit.

No. 43076, 31 May 1997
No. 43076, unusually, works through Washwood Heath heading for Birmingham New Street, wearing Midland Mainline teal livery. This must have been on hire to Virgin Trains CrossCountry at the time.

No. 43077, 21 April 2004
No. 43077 arrives at a gloomy Chesterfield with a working to Sheffield, carrying Midland Mainline livery. Of note is that the Mk3 carriages have already been repainted into the new livery of grey and white, although the power cars still retain the old livery. No. 43077 has since been renumbered as 43277 following fitting of an MTU power unit, and operates on the east coast.

No. 43078, 4 June 2005

No. 43078 stands at Newton Abbott while on loan from GNER to Virgin Trains CrossCountry for summer Saturday services. These moves regularly brought East Coast HSTs to the southwest and the sight of GNER-liveried Class 43s far from their traditional stamping ground. No. 43078 was only used by GNER for about twelve months before going to First Great Western.

No. 43078, 22 May 2008

No. 43078 is seen departing Bristol Temple Meads on the back of a First Great Western through working from the south-west to London Paddington. This power car had come to First from the east coast.

No. 43080, 20 March 2003

No. 43080 is seen departing Doncaster, carrying Virgin Trains livery, which certainly brightened up the appearance of the power cars. This is another Class 43 carrying buffers and draw gear. This would later pass to Grand Central.

No. 43080, 24 March 2009

No. 43080 arrives at London King's Cross carrying Grand Central livery. Grand Central started operating in 2007, and serves Bradford and Sunderland from London King's Cross.

No. 43081, 19 June 1999

No. 43081 is seen carrying Midland Mainline teal livery on the back of a working to London St Pancras at Sheffield.

Nos 43082 and 43055, 27 March 1998

Nos 43082 and 43055 are seen side by side at London St Pancras showing the distinctive nose detail of the Class 43. Both power cars wear Midland Mainline teal livery, a scheme that really suited the class.

No. 43082, 29 January 2013

No. 43082 is seen at Nottingham having arrived with a terminating service from London St Pancras. The loco carries the current East Midlands Trains livery, and also the name *Railway Children The Voice For Street Children Worldwide*.

No. 43083, 1 April 2008

No. 43083 rests at Nottingham, having arrived from London St Pancras. The loco carries the second version of Midland Mainline livery, although the wording has been removed as the franchise had changed to East Midlands Trains by this time.

No. 43084, 24 February 1987

No. 43084 *County of Derbyshire* is seen making a station call at Peterborough, while wearing InterCity executive livery. This would later go to Stratford for conversion to a buffer-fitted example.

No. 43084, 24 March 2009

No. 43084 is seen at London King's Cross carrying the original Grand Central livery of plain black. The later version would include an orange stripe.

No. 43087, 17 November 2008

No. 43087 is seen at Cardiff Central waiting to depart with a First Great Western working to London Paddington. In the next few years, the First Great Western Class 43s will disappear, being replaced by the Hitachi-built Class 800 InterCity Express units.

No. 43088, 10 August 1988

No. 43088 departs Leeds for London King's Cross wearing InterCity executive livery. The power car carries the name *XIII Commonwealth Games Scotland 1986*, which it carried for four years.

No. 43091, 2 April 2009

No. 43091 is seen at Bristol Temple Meads on the rear of a terminating First Great Western service from London Paddington. There are plans for some of the First Great Western Class 43s to move to Scotrail when they have been replaced by the Class 800s.

No. 43092, 12 March 2015

No. 43092 is seen arriving at London Paddington with a high-speed working from the south-west, a scene which has occurred almost daily for the past forty years. No. 43092 carries First Great Western blue livery.

No. 43093, 23 October 1998

No. 43093 is seen making a station call at Doncaster, carrying Virgin Trains CrossCountry livery, and also the name *Lady in Red*. The XC logo on the side would be removed not long after, leaving just the Virgin branding.

No. 43095, 13 April 1985

No. 43095 stands at Derby carrying original InterCity 125 blue and yellow livery. This power car also carries the name *Heaton*, and is seen waiting to depart for London St Pancras. No. 43095 now carries the number 43295 and has been fitted with an MTU power unit.

No. 43097, 11 April 1990

No. 43097 stands at Derby having just been released from works, carrying InterCity swallow livery complete with large numbers on the front. Of note is the fact that the Mk3 carriages still carry their original blue-and-grey livery.

No. 43098, 1 June 1988

No. 43098 departs Leeds for London King's Cross carrying InterCity swallow livery. This was another livery that suited the Class 43s.

Nos 43099 and 43013, 27 August 2002

Nos 43099 and 43013 are seen back to back at Totnes while undergoing a test run from Laira depot. Both locos carry Virgin Trains livery, and this was a regular way to test power cars before release to traffic, following repairs. No. 43099 has since been renumbered as 43299, following the fitting of an MTU power unit, and now works for Virgin Trains East Coast.

No. 43100, 13 June 1998

No. 43100 is seen at Sheffield carrying Virgin Trains livery and also the name *Blackpool Rock*. This name was unusual at the time, in that it was a sticker rather than a cast nameplate – a practice that has become more prevalent in recent years. No. 43100 has been renumbered as 43300 and now works for Virgin Trains East Coast.

No. 43100, 31 May 2002

No. 43100 is seen at Plymouth coupled to No. 08644. This power car had been removed from a Virgin Trains rake in the platform and was about to be taken back to Laira for attention. No. 43100 has since been fitted with an MTU power unit and has been renumbered as 43300, working the East Coast route for Virgin Trains East Coast.

No. 43101, 24 August 1984

No. 43101 is seen making a typically smoky Valenta departure from Leeds, heading for London King's Cross. The power car carries the name *Edinburgh International Festival*, and it had only been named the previous day. This is how I remember the Class 43s: at their best in BR blue-and-yellow livery. This loco is still in use today with CrossCountry Trains, but has been renumbered as 43301.

No. 43102, 14 May 2004

No. 43102 is seen stabled at Derby Etches Park, carrying unbranded Virgin Trains livery. This had finished use with Virgin Trains in 2003, and is seen when on hire to Midland Mainline. No. 43102 has since had an MTU engine fitted, and has been renumbered as 43302, working for Virgin Trains East Coast.

No. 43104, 6 October 1998

No. 43104 is seen stored at Plymouth Laira carrying InterCity Swallow livery and also the name *County of Cleveland*. This would spend approximately five years out of use, before being put back into service with Virgin Trains CrossCountry. It has since been renumbered as 43304 following the fitting of an MTU power unit.

No. 43104, 20 April 2002

No. 43104 is seen at Birmingham International carrying Virgin Trains red livery. This power car spent many years out of use at Laira depot, before being put back into service with Virgin Trains, and also carries the name *City of Edinburgh*. No. 43104 has since been renumbered as 43304, having had an MTU power unit fitted.

No. 43105, 8 June 1987

No. 43105 passes Saltley depot, Birmingham, carrying InterCity executive livery and heading for the north-east. This power car also carries the name *Hartlepool*. No. 43105 now carries the number 43305, and has had an MTU power unit fitted, replacing the Paxman Valenta engine.

No. 43105, 13 August 2004

No. 43105 is seen at Doncaster carrying GNER livery and the name *Inverness*. After privatisation, GNER were quick to apply their livery across their fleet, and No. 43105 carries the later gold GNER logo, whereas the earlier recipients had a white logo. No. 43105 now carries the number 43305.

No. 43107, 24 August 1983

No. 43107 is seen making a station call at Doncaster, carrying BR blue-and-yellow livery. This power car also carries its running number on the front, and is one of a batch of locos that spent their entire life working the east coast, right up to present day. No. 43107 has since been renumbered as 43307, following the fitting of an MTU engine.

No. 43109, 26 February 1988

No. 43109 is seen passing Washwood Heath, Birmingham, carrying InterCity executive livery and heading for Birmingham New Street. The gasholders and industrial estate in the background have both since been demolished. No. 43109 now carries the number 43309, having had an MTU power unit fitted.

No. 43110, 6 April 1997

No. 43110 is seen at Newcastle station carrying freshly applied GNER blue livery with an orange stripe. The loco also carries a white GNER logo, which would be replaced with a gold version. No. 43110 has since been renumbered as 43310, having had an MTU power unit installed.

No. 43110, 18 October 2004

No. 43110 stands at London King's Cross waiting to depart with a working to the north via the East Coast Main Line. No. 43110 carries GNER livery, and has had its white GNER logo replaced with a gold version, and also carries the name *Stirlingshire*. When the East Coast fleet was re-engined with MTU power units, they were renumbered, with 43110 becoming 43310.

No. 43111, 2 August 2007

No. 43111 is seen arriving at Peterborough in GNER blue livery with a matching rake of Mk3 carriages. The arrival of the Class 43s on the east coast helped eliminate the popular Deltics from this route. No. 43111 now carries the running number 43311, following the fitting of an MTU engine.

No. 43112, 7 September 2000

No. 43112 is seen at Derby carrying GNER livery. This power car was on hire to Midland Mainline at the time, hence its appearance at Derby. It would go on to receive the name *Doncaster*. This has now been renumbered as 43312, having had its Paxman Valenta engine replaced with an MTU power unit.

No. 43113, 13 August 2004

No. 43113 is seen arriving at Doncaster, carrying GNER livery. This livery looked good on the Class 43s, but the positioning of the number was strange, being in blue at the end of the orange stripe. No. 43113 carries the name *The Highlands*, and has since been renumbered as 43313.

No. 43114, 9 May 2006

No. 43114 arrives at Doncaster on the back of a GNER working from London King's Cross. The loco carries the name *East Riding of Yorkshire*, and has since been renumbered as 43314 following the fitting of an MTU power unit. The East Coast fleet is due for replacement, with Hitachi-built Class 800 InterCity Express units taking over. The East Coast won't be the same without the Class 43s, in the same way as the LNER A4s and the Class 55 Deltics before them.

No. 43115, 3 September 2005

No. 43115 is seen in GNER livery at Newton Abbot while on hire to Virgin Trains CrossCountry for summer Saturday workings to the southwest. These workings saw the unusual sight of GNER examples enjoying a day off the east coast. No. 43115 carries the name *Aberdeenshire*, and has since been renumbered as 43315, following the fitting of an MTU engine.

No. 43116, 30 March 1997

No. 43116 approaches Thirsk, North Yorkshire, with a GNER working to London King's Cross. Both power cars carry the then-new GNER livery, but the Mk3 carriages still carry InterCity livery. No. 43116 has since been renumbered as 43316, having had an MTU power unit installed.

No. 43122, 4 September 1994

No. 43122 stands at Newcastle carrying InterCity swallow livery. This power car also carries the name *South Yorkshire Metropolitan County*.

No. 43126, 4 August 1996

No. 43126 rests at Swansea Maliphant sidings carrying InterCity swallow livery. This power car also carries the name *City of Bristol*.

No. 43127, 2 June 2000

No. 43127 stands at Exeter St Davids, waiting to depart for London Paddington with a First Great Western working. This power car carries the second version of the First Great Western livery, one that sits a little awkwardly on the power car and was, thankfully, changed.

No. 43128, 29 June 1991

No. 43128 is seen under repair at Bristol Bath Road during the open day of 1991. The power car is seen on the jacks, having had its bogies removed, and carries InterCity swallow livery. Unfortunately, this depot has since been closed and demolished.

Nos 43128, 43165 and 43151, 12 March 2015

Nos 43128, 43165 and 43151 are seen side by side at London Paddington in the classic pose from that location. All three power cars have been fitted with MTU engines and, unlike their CrossCountry and East Coast counterparts, still retain their original running numbers.

No. 43129, 1 April 1997

No. 43129 is seen at Cardiff Central, having arrived from London Paddington. This loco carries the first version of Great Western livery, which looked quite pleasing on the class.

No. 43130, 12 August 1987

No. 43130 is seen arriving at Penzance, carrying InterCity executive livery. This power car also carries the set number 253030 on the front, although this practice wouldn't last long due to power cars being swapped between sets.

No. 43130, 5 June 1997

No. 43130 waits to depart from Cardiff Central with a Great Western working to London Paddington. Of note is the fact that the Mk3 carriages have already been repainted into Great Western livery, but the loco still carries InterCity swallow livery. No. 43130 also carries the name *Sulis Minerva*.

No. 43132, 1 March 1997

No. 43132 is seen standing at London Paddington, waiting to depart for the south-west. The loco carries Great Western livery, but the Mk3 carriages still retain InterCity livery. The power car had recently lost its *Worshipful Company of Carmen* nameplates.

No. 43133, 30 January 1999

No. 43133 is seen in Great Western livery, having arrived at a very gloomy Swansea with a Great Western working from London Paddington. This power car has worked the Great Western route all its life, having only been allocated to Old Oak Common, St Phillip's Marsh, Landore and Laira in thirty-five years.

No. 43134, 22 May 2008

No. 43134 is seen at Bristol Temple Meads, having arrived with a terminating service from London Paddington. The loco carries First Great Western blue livery, having had an MTU power unit fitted. The building in the background is the old Royal Mail sorting terminal, which closed when the railway stopped carrying letters and parcels.

No. 43137, 20 August 1998

No. 43137 stands at Plymouth station waiting to depart for London Paddington. The loco carries the first version of Great Western livery, and also carries the name *Newton Abbot 150*.

No. 43139, 26 May 2004

No. 43139 is seen at Plymouth during the transition from the second version of First Great Western livery to the newer blue version. The Mk3 carriages had already been repainted, but No. 43139 was still to be completed.

No. 43140, 22 May 2008

No. 43140 is seen departing Bristol Temple Meads on the back of a First Great Western working to London Paddington. The class has been synonymous with the Western route for nearly forty years, and their replacements are due within a couple of years.

No. 43142, 26 July 2002

No. 43142 is seen at Plymouth carrying First Great Western blue-and-gold livery, and also carries the white front. The white would be replaced with blue, being easier to keep clean. This power car once carried the name *St Mary's Hospital, Paddington*.

No. 43143, 10 August 1992

No. 43143 stands at Plymouth station, having arrived from London Paddington. At the time, this was the corporate InterCity swallow livery carried by all Class 43 power cars.

No. 43144, 29 June 1991

No. 43144 stands at Bristol Temple Meads having arrived with a working to London Paddington from the south-west. The loco carries InterCity swallow livery.

No. 43144, 22 May 2008

No. 43144 departs from Bristol Temple Meads on the back of a First Great Western working to London Paddington. The loco carries First blue livery, having had an MTU engine fitted.

No. 43148, 22 May 2008

No. 43148 is seen arriving at Bristol Temple Meads with a First Great Western working from London Paddington to the south-west. The loco carries the attractive plain blue First Great Western livery.

No. 43151, 26 June 1990

No. 43151 is seen being dragged past Washwood Heath by No. 31248, heading back towards the Western Region. The loco is separated from the Class 31 by a converted BG, which has been converted into a HST barrier vehicle, and some of these carriages are still in use today. No. 43151 carries InterCity swallow livery, and also has a tail lamp fitted on the nose.

No. 43152, 31 May 1981

No. 43152 is seen here when brand new at Coalville open day 1981. This loco had yet to turn a wheel in revenue-earning service; it wasn't delivered to Old Oak Common until a few weeks later. Of note is the 'W' prefix before the running number, indicating a Western Region example, and it also carries the set number 253041 on the coupling cover.

No. 43152, 26 November 2001

No. 43152 is seen at Newport waiting to depart for London Paddington. This power car carries the second version of First Great Western livery, with the gold band. I was not a big fan of this livery and, thankfully, it was replaced with the blue-and-gold version.

No. 43155, 30 August 2001

No. 43155 is seen at Plymouth station with No. 43004 coupling up to it. No. 43004 had been taken off a First Great Western set in the station, with its replacement No. 43185 being attached. No. 43155 was used to bring the replacement power car from Laira, and would be used to take No. 43004 back. This practice happened quite often at Plymouth, although the use of a Virgin Trains power car with a First Great Western loco was unusual. No. 43155 carries the name *City of Aberdeen*.

No. 43156, 13 June 1995

No. 43156 is seen powering south through Water Orton on the outskirts of Birmingham, carrying InterCity swallow livery. HSTs still work through Water Orton today – usually CrossCountry-liveried examples.

No. 43158, 25 October 1996

No. 43158 is seen making a station call at Doncaster with an InterCity CrossCountry working to the south-west. The loco carries the name *Dartmoor, The Pony Express,* and would soon pass to Virgin Trains CrossCountry, who took over these services in January 1997.

No. 43162, 4 August 1996

No. 43162 is seen arriving at Cardiff Central with a complete InterCity-liveried rake of Mk3 carriages. The loco carries the name *Borough of Stevenage*, but is one of the replacements for the cast versions, made of tin instead. No. 43162 would transfer to Virgin Trains CrossCountry at the beginning of 1997.

No. 43162, 21 September 1999

No. 43162 is seen carrying Virgin Trains CrossCountry livery at Southampton Central. Many of the Virgin Class 43s were replaced with Class 220 Voyager units, with No. 43162 passing to Midland Mainline as part of their Project Rio, before finally passing to First Great Western.

No. 43168, 22 March 1986

No. 43168 is seen departing Crewe while still carrying BR blue-and-yellow InterCity 125 livery. This was one of four power cars experimentally fitted with a Mirrlees MB190 engine in the late 1980s; however, these were to prove unsuccessful, and it was later fitted with a Paxman VP185 instead. This was later replaced with an MTU power unit.

Nos 43169 and 43183, 27 March 1998

Nos 43169 and 43183 are seen side by side at London Paddington, both carrying the first version of Great Western livery. No. 43169 was one of four power cars fitted with a Mirrlees MB190 engine, although it was to prove so problematic that the power car would be stored for four years, before finally being fitted with a Paxman VP185 and re-entering service. It was later fitted with an MTU power unit, like the rest of the Great Western fleet. No. 43169 carries the name *The National Trust*.

No. 43170, 2 April 2009

No. 43170 is seen departing Bristol Temple Meads on the back of a First Great Western working to London Paddington. This was the last of a quartet of power cars fitted with a Mirrlees MB190 power unit in the late 1980s; the engine was not a success and, after spending many years out of service, they were all fitted with Paxman VP185 engines. However, as part of the First Great Western re-engineering project, it was fitted with an MTU engine. At one time, this power car was named *Edward Paxman*, although the name was later removed.

No. 43171, 15 August 1988

No. 43171 is seen passing through Northallerton, North Yorkshire, on the back of rake of blue-and-grey Mk3 carriages. The power also carries the set number 253045 on the front. The set number 253 related to the Western Region and CrossCountry sets, whereas the Scottish and Eastern Regions had set numbers starting with 254, but both were removed after power cars swapped sets. No. 253045 related to a CrossCountry set.

No. 43172, 21 April 1987

No. 43172 is seen departing Leeds on the back of a CrossCountry working, while carrying BR blue-and-yellow InterCity 125 livery. At the time, this was one of the last power cars to carry this livery, with most being painted into InterCity executive livery, and some straight into InterCity swallow livery.

No. 43172, 17 November 2008

No. 43172 is seen arriving at Cardiff Central, carrying First Great Western blue livery. This livery was carried when the locos were fitted with new MTU engines.

No. 43174, 11 May 2003

No. 43174 is seen passing Totnes wearing the green-and-gold First Great Western livery. This power car was named *Bristol–Bordeaux*.

No. 43176, 3 May 1983

No. 43176 is seen passing Saltley, coupled back to back with No. 43175, while on a test run from Derby Works, despite the power cars only being eighteen months old. Testing of power cars in this way was a regular occurrence at the time.

No. 43177, 29 August 1991

No. 43177 is seen at Plymouth station, having been brought from Laira depot by No. 47473 for swapping onto an InterCity working. No. 43177 carries InterCity executive livery and would replace No. 43179, which would come off the rake of Mk3 carriages.

No. 43179, 29 August 1991

No. 43179 is seen at Plymouth station, having been uncoupled from a rake of Mk3 carriages. The power car was being replaced with No. 43177, and No. 43179 would return to Laira for attention. No. 43179 would be repainted and, two weeks later at Laira open day, would be named *Pride of Laira*. This view shows the gangway connection between power car and carriages, and also the coupling between them as well.

No. 43179, 5 June 1997

No. 43179 is seen arriving at Newport, carrying Great Western green-and-ivory livery. Note how the carriages have yet to be repainted, still carrying InterCity livery. No. 43179 carries the name *Pride of Laira*.

No. 43180, 7 January 1985

No. 43180 is seen most unusually parked at Lawley Street container terminal, Birmingham. The power car still carries InterCity 125 blue-and-yellow livery. It was never common to see locos stabled at Lawley Street, never mind Class 43s.

No. 43180, 29 June 1991

No. 43180 is seen on display at St Phillip's Marsh depot open day 1991. The loco carries InterCity swallow livery, which was standard for the HST fleet at the time. Both Bristol depots, St Phillip's Marsh and Bath Road had an open day on the same day.

No. 43180, 2 September 1994

No. 43180 is seen in storage at Edinburgh Craigentinny depot with collision damage. The loco had been hit by No. 37113 just outside Edinburgh. The damage resulted in the Class 37 being scrapped, whereas No. 43180 was repaired at Crewe Works but was out of use for two years.

No. 43182, 22 May 2008

No. 43182 is seen arriving at Bristol Temple Meads with a terminating service from London Paddington. The loco carries blue First Great Western livery, which it received following the fitting of its MTU engine.

No. 43185, 5 June 1997

No. 43185 is seen at Cardiff Central waiting to depart with a Great Western working to London Paddington. The loco carries Great Western livery, and also carries the name *Great Western*.

No. 43185, 30 August 2001

No. 43185 is seen being backed onto a rake of Mk3 carriages following a power car swap in the station. The defective power car, No. 43004, had been removed, allowing No. 43185 to attach to the carriages. No. 43185 carries the name *Great Western*.

No. 43188, 30 January 1999

No. 43188 is seen arriving at a gloomy Swansea station after the long run from London Paddington. The loco carries Great Western livery and carries the name *City of Plymouth*.

No. 43190, 31 July 1982

No. 43190 is seen departing Birmingham New Street while carrying BR blue-and-yellow InterCity 125 livery. This power car had only been released from Crewe Works a couple of months before. Unusually, it carries the name *Heart Line* above the windscreen, which adorned just a handful of the class when they took over the north-east–south-west route from the Class 45s.

No. 43190, 26 May 2007

No. 43190 is seen departing Newton Abbot with a First Great Western working to London Paddington. The loco carries the blue-and-gold version of First Great Western livery, which sat nicely on the locos and stock, replacing the blue-and-white livery. When fitted with an MTU engine, it would be painted all over blue.

No. 43191, 31 August 1984

No. 43191 is seen at Crewe still carrying BR blue-and-yellow InterCity 125 livery. This was at a time when parcels were still carried by British Rail, and No. 43191 has arrived at Crewe with quite a few sacks of mail and parcels.

No. 43191, 8 March 1997

No. 43191 is an unusual sight passing Washwood Heath, Birmingham, heading for the Northeast. The loco and rake of Mk3 carriages carry Great Western livery; this is the only time I've seen a Great Western-liveried HST working this far north, and it was presumably on hire to Virgin Trains CrossCountry. No. 43191 carries the name *Seahawk*.

No. 43192, 12 March 2015

No. 43192 is seen at London Paddington carrying plain First Great Western blue livery in a scene that has been repeated for nearly forty years. The loco had been fitted with an MTU power unit by this time, hence the plain blue livery.

No. 43193, 30 August 1985

No. 43193 is seen at Leeds carrying InterCity executive livery. The loco carries the name *Yorkshire Post*, which it had for eight years.

No. 43193, 30 August 1996

No. 43193 is seen waiting to depart from Carlisle station, carrying InterCity Swallow livery. This loco had been named *Yorkshire Post*, but these plates were removed and the loco was renamed *Plymouth City of Discovery*.

No. 43197, 18 October 2004

No. 43197 is seen at London King's Cross, carrying recently applied GNER livery. This power car spent time in and out of service, being hired to various TOCs before finally finding a home with First Great Western, receiving an MTU engine in the process.

No. 43198, 3 August 1999

No. 43198 is seen at Birmingham International on the rear of a Virgin Trains CrossCountry working, heading for Bournemouth. This was the last Class 43 to be built at Crewe Works, and was released six years after the first power car.

No. 43206, 27 November 2008

No. 43206 is seen at London King's Cross carrying a mismatch of liveries. The loco is in former GNER blue livery, but the orange stripe has been replaced with a full-length white stripe and National Express wording. The Mk3 carriages carry the new National Express East Coast livery of white and silver. No. 43206 was renumbered from 43006 when it was fitted with an MTU power unit.

No. 43206, 12 June 2012

No. 43206 is seen arriving at London King's Cross, carrying East Coast livery. The East Coast franchise had temporarily gone back into public ownership following National Express ownership, but the franchise would be re-let back into private ownership, with it being run by Virgin Trains East Coast. In the interim, the locos and stock were painted into East Coast livery of all-over grey. The Mk3 carriages in the photograph had come from East Midlands Trains, and carried East Coast logos. No. 43206 was renumbered from 43006 when it was fitted with an MTU engine.

No. 43208, 16 September 2015

No. 43208 is seen arriving at Edinburgh Waverley with a Virgin Trains East Coast working to London King's Cross. The loco carries former East Coast livery of all-over grey, but with Virgin branding applied over the top of the grey. It also carries the name *Lincolnshire Echo*, and was renumbered from 43008 when it was fitted with an MTU power unit.

No. 43251, 6 August 2009

No. 43251 is seen powering north through Doncaster on the back of a National Express East Coast working. The loco and coaching stock is in full National Express livery, except for the carriage next to No. 43251; this still carries former GNER blue livery, but the orange stripe has been replaced with a white stripe. No. 43251 was renumbered from 43051 when it had an MTU engine fitted.

No. 43257, 24 March 2009

No. 43257 is seen arriving at London King's Cross, carrying National Express East Coast livery. When fitted with an MTU power unit, No. 43257 was renumbered from 43057.

No. 43277, 6 August 2009

No. 43277 is seen departing Doncaster with a National Express East Coast working to London King's Cross. The loco carries full National Express livery, and was renumbered from 43077 when it was fitted with an MTU power unit.

No. 43277, 19 March 2013

No. 43277 is seen at London King's Cross. By this time, it has lost its National Express East Coast livery and now carries plain East Coast grey livery. Along with the rest of the East Coast fleet, it will gain Virgin Trains red livery. No. 43277 was renumbered from 43077 when it was fitted with an MTU engine.

No. 43285, 23 July 2012

No. 43285 is seen working south through Longbridge station in the Birmingham suburbs. This loco carries CrossCountry livery, and is one of ten such locos to carry these colours. No. 43285 was renumbered from 43085 when it was fitted with an MTU power unit.

No. 43290, 25 May 2007

No. 43290 is seen at Newton Abbot, carrying GNER livery. The loco also carries advertising for the Leeds–London service, looking somewhat out of place in South Devon. The loco was on hire to Virgin Trains CrossCountry, for use on summer Saturday extra services to the south-west. No. 43290 also carries the name *MTU Fascination of Power*, and was renumbered from No. 43090 when it had an MTU power unit fitted, being one of the first East Coast locos so treated.

No. 43290, 6 August 2009

No. 43290 is seen approaching Doncaster, carrying National Express East Coast livery. National Express only ran the East Coast franchise for just under two years before defaulting on its payments, and the franchise came back into public ownership, meaning the locos only wore the livery in its full form with branding for a short time. No. 43290 carries the name *MTU Fascination of Power*, and was renumbered from 43090 when it had an MTU power unit fitted.

No. 43295, 12 June 2012

No. 43295 stands at London King's Cross before departing north once again. The loco carries former operator National Express East Coast livery, but has had the logos removed and East Coast logos applied over the top of the livery. It would later be painted into East Coast grey livery, before finally being painted into Virgin Trains East Coast red livery. Some Class 43 locos have carried four different liveries over a short seven-year period. No. 43295 was renumbered from 43095 when it was fitted with an MTU power unit.

No. 43299, 18 September 2015

No. 43299 is seen departing Haymarket station, Edinburgh, with a working to the north of Scotland. The loco carries the new Virgin Trains East Coast livery of red and grey. Despite the name, Virgin only own 10 per cent of the company, with Stagecoach group owning the majority. No. 43299 was renumbered from 43099 when it was fitted with an MTU power unit.

No. 43300, 12 June 2012

No. 43300 is seen having arrived at London King's Cross with a working from Scotland. No. 43300 carries the full East Coast livery of all over grey with East Coast branding, whereas the MK3 carriages still carry the livery of former operator, National Express East Coast. No. 43300 carries the name *Craigentinny* after the depot in Edinburgh, which looks after both the East Coast fleet, as well as the CrossCountry fleet. No. 43300 was renumbered from 43100.

No. 43300, 10 March 2015

No. 43300 is seen basking in the sun at Leeds, waiting to depart south towards London King's Cross. The loco carries the all-over grey base livery of its former operator, East Coast, but has had Virgin branding applied over the top. The loco also carries special logos celebrating 100 years of Craigentinny depot in Edinburgh. No. 43300 also carries the name *Craigentinny* and, by this time, had had a special plaque unveiled on top of the nameplate. The Mk3 carriages still carry National Express East Coast livery, despite them not running the franchise since 2009. When No. 43300 was fitted with an MTU engine, it was renumbered from 43100.

No. 43301, 19 September 2015

No. 43301 stands at Edinburgh Waverley with a CrossCountry working to the south-west. No. 43301 is one of ten such power cars in use with CrossCountry, and was renumbered from 43101 when it was fitted with an MTU engine. Edinburgh is a good place to see Class 43s, with both CrossCountry and Virgin Trains East Coast examples working through the station.

No. 43303, 25 January 2013

No. 43303 brings up the rear of a CrossCountry working at Water Orton during the winter of 2013. No. 43303 was renumbered from 43103 when it was fitted with an MTU engine. It is a testament to the design that the HST is still providing the backbone of high-speed diesel trains in the UK, forty years after they were first introduced.

No. 43305, 27 November 2008

No. 43305 stands at London King's Cross waiting to depart with another East Coast Main Line working. The loco carries National Express East Coast livery; National Express operated the East Coast franchise for a short two-year period. No. 43305 was originally numbered 43105, but became No. 43305 when it had an MTU engine fitted.

No. 43309, 16 September 2015

No. 43309 is seen making a station call at Haymarket station, Edinburgh. The loco carries new Virgin Trains East Coast red livery, and this livery is certainly a lot brighter than the former East Coast grey livery. The East Coast fleet is scheduled for replacement, with Hitachi building the Class 800 InterCity Express units to replace them. No. 43309 was renumbered from 43109 when it had an MTU power unit fitted.

No. 43311, 12 June 2012

No. 43311 is seen as it arrives at London King's Cross on the back of an East Coast working from the north. No. 43311 carries full East Coast livery of all-over grey. The Mk3 carriages with it carry East Midlands Trains livery, but have East Coast logos applied, following transfer from EMT. No. 43311 was renumbered from 43111 when the MTU power unit was fitted, replacing the Paxman Valenta engine.

No. 43313, 24 March 2009

No. 43313 stands on the buffer stops at London King's Cross, complete with 'not to be moved' board attached. No. 43313 carries former operator GNER livery of all-over blue, but the orange stripe has been replaced by a white stripe with National Express written on it. No. 43313 was originally numbered 43113, but was renumbered to 43313 when an MTU engine was fitted.

No. 43314, 29 June 2015

No. 43314 is seen passing through Alexander Palace on the back of a Virgin Trains East Coast working to London King's Cross. The loco carries former East Coast livery, but with Virgin Trains branding added over the top of it, although the MK3 carriages still retain full East Coast livery. No. 43314 was renumbered from 43114 when fitted with an MTU power unit.

No. 43316, 22 March 2013

No. 43316 departs from London King's Cross on the back of an East Coast working. No. 43316 carries full East Coast livery, along with the Mk3 carriages, but has lost its running number from the coupling cover on the front. Originally numbered 43116, it would become No. 43316 during the MTU-engine-replacement programme.

No. 43317, 12 June 2012

No. 43317 is seen departing London King's Cross on the back of an East Coast working. The loco and Mk3 carriages still retain the livery of former operator National Express, but with East Coast logos placed over the top of the livery. No. 43317 was renumbered from 43117 when it was fitted with an MTU engine.

No. 43318, 27 November 2008

No. 43318 stands at London King's Cross waiting to depart with a service to the north. No. 43318 carries its former GNER livery, but with a white stripe covering the orange stripe and 'National Express' written on the white. National Express had been operating the East Coast franchise for nearly twelve months, but would only run it for a further twelve months before the route passed to public ownership. No. 43318 was renumbered from 43118 when it was fitted with an MTU power unit.

No. 43318, 17 September 2015

No. 43318 is seen arriving at Perth with a Virgin Trains East Coast working to Inverness from London King's Cross, a journey of just over eight hours. No. 43318 carries the latest Virgin Trains East Coast red livery, and was renumbered from 43118 when it was fitted with an MTU engine.

No. 43319, 6 August 2009

No. 43319 stands at Doncaster waiting to depart for London King's Cross, carrying full National Express livery, despite them only running the franchise for another four months. Doncaster has always been a good place to see Class 43s at work, with East Coast and CrossCountry examples working through the station, both stopping and at high speed. No. 43319 was renumbered from 43119 when the MTU power unit was fitted, replacing the Paxman Valenta.

No. 43321, 31 December 2012

No. 43321 stands waiting to depart from Derby with a CrossCountry working to the south-west. The loco carries CrossCountry livery and, despite there only being five CrossCountry sets in traffic, they certainly cover some miles. Derby is another good place to see Class 43s at work with East Midlands Trains, CrossCountry and Network Rail examples working through the station. No. 43321 was renumbered from 43121 when it had an MTU power unit fitted.

No. 43321, 27 March 2013

No. 43321 is seen approaching a snowy Longbridge station, in the south-west Birmingham suburbs, with a CrossCountry working to Plymouth. No. 43321 was originally numbered 43121, but was renumbered when it had an MTU engine fitted.

No. 43384, 28 August 2012

No. 43384 is seen powering north through Water Orton on the back of a CrossCountry working to the north-east. Class 43s have been associated with the north-east–south-west route from the early 1980s, and there are currently no plans to replace these locos on the route. No. 43384 was renumbered from 43184 when it was overhauled and fitted with an MTU power unit.

No. 43384, 10 June 2015

No. 43384 is seen approaching Longbridge station, Birmingham, from the south-west with a CrossCountry working to the northeast. The train has not long come up the notorious Lickey Incline, which is the UK's steepest gradient at 1 in 37.7 for two miles, just north of Bromsgrove station. No. 43384 was renumbered from 43184 when fitted with an MTU engine.

No. 43484, 29 June 2015

No. 43484 is seen standing at London King's Cross, carrying the new Grand Central livery. No. 43484 also carries the name *Peter Fox 1942–2011 Platform 5*. There are currently six Class 43 power cars working for Grand Central, and all are based at Heaton depot, Newcastle. All have been fitted with MTU engines, including No. 43484, which was renumbered from 43084 during the process.